I0624305

# *Pray*
## FOR HIM
### PRAYER JOURNAL
PRAYING FOR YOUR PASTOR-HUSBAND
EXPANDED EDITION

**FAITH PUBLICATIONS**

ISBN: 978-1-960820-05-1 (paperback)
ISBN: 978-1-960820-06-8 (digital)

First printing edition 2024

Faith Publications
1900 NW 4th St.
Ankeny, IA 50023

faith.edu/publications

Pray for Him Prayer Journal
Praying for Your Pastor-Husband
Expanded Edition

Previous edition published in 2013 as *Pray for Him: Praying for
Your Pastor-Husband.*

Unless otherwise noted, all Scripture quotations are from the
New King James Version®. Copyright © 1982 by Thomas Nelson.
Used by permission. All rights reserved.

Cover Image by iStock.com/Wirestock

Cover and Interior Design by Natalie C. Aeschliman

Printed in the United States of America

To pastors' wives everywhere who are
striving to help their pastor-husbands
faithfully fulfill their God-given calling

You also helping together in prayer for me, that thanks may be given by many persons on my behalf for the gift granted to me through many.

2 Corinthians 1:11

## Dear Pastor's Wife:

In 2 Corinthians 1:11 Paul tells the church at Corinth that they can help him in his ministry by praying for him. As helpmeets to pastors, we have the incredible privilege and responsibility to help our husbands in their ministries by praying for them.

I hope and pray that this simple resource will help you be a helper to him through a ministry of prayer.

In Him,

Faith Taylor

# Contents

# Why You Should Pray for Your Pastor-Husband

As a young pastor's wife, I understood that God had called me to be my husband's helper, but I wrestled with how to best help him in the ministry God had called him to. I feared saying or doing the wrong thing, and I struggled with the weight of the expectations others had placed on me and that I had put on myself.

How do you view your role as a pastor's wife? How can you best support your pastor-husband and complement him in his calling?

As you evaluate your role, please consider the following suggestions:

- **Use your gifts in the church, but don't try to be the assistant pastor.**

  "How is your wife planning to serve in the church?" This typical question was asked of my husband both times he candidated for a lead pastorate.

For decades (if not centuries), expectations have been placed on a pastor's wife about the ways she should contribute to her husband's pastoral ministry: she should be musical; she should be a gifted Bible teacher; she should be a great biblical counselor, an event planner, and the queen of hospitality.

These expectations may creep into your own thinking, causing you to conclude that your contribution to your husband's ministry hinges on fulfilling these expectations.

If God has gifted you in any of the above-listed areas, by all means use those gifts to faithfully serve in the church—not because you are the pastor's wife, but because you are a contributing member of the body of Christ. This is the responsibility of every member of the body of Christ (Rom 12:3–8; 1 Cor 12; Eph 4:7–16).

So serve the Lord with your gifts, but remember that you are not the assistant pastor. The success of the ministry does not depend on all the ways you may serve. You perhaps feel pressured to do, do, and do some more to help your husband succeed, but the use of your gifts is not the greatest way you will help your husband in his ministry.

I would suggest, rather, that you have the opportunity to make a greater contribution.

● **Recognize that one of your greatest contributions to your husband's ministry is prayer.**

In 2 Corinthians 1:11 Paul expresses the church's obligation to help the apostles in their ministry through prayer. He recognized their desperate need for the power of God and depended on the prayers of God's people.

All the members of the body of Christ should participate in the ministry of the church through prayer. As the wife of the pastor, however, you have the greatest vantage point to be able to pray for him specifically. You are one with him, and you know him best. You have a front-row seat to the weaknesses he feels, to the challenges he faces, and to the burdens that he bears. That knowledge enables you to pray fervently for him.

You can and should pray for him as no one else can or should.

Your faithful prayers for your pastor-husband

accomplish more than the use of any gift you may have. Why? Because your husband is on the frontline of spiritual warfare.

In Ephesians 6 Paul addresses the spiritual warfare every believer is engaged in and exhorts Christians to put on the armor of God. He ends the passage with an instruction to be "praying always" for those in ministry (Eph 6:18–20). Prayer is vital to one's successful involvement in spiritual warfare.

First Peter 5:8 describes the devil as a roaring lion, prowling around seeking whom he can devour. Interestingly, if you look at verse 1 of this chapter, you will see that Peter is specifically addressing the elders (i.e., the pastors) of the church. While Satan's destructive efforts are not limited to pastors, I believe this passage indicates that they are a primary target. If Satan can hinder or destroy a pastor's ministry, he can potentially hinder or destroy all the members of that local body. The ramifications of the pastor's failure are multiplied.

God desires that you use your gifts to serve in the church as a member of the body of Christ, but as the helper of your pastor-husband, you have the vital role of upholding your husband in prayer. And with the knowledge you have of him, you can powerfully intercede for him before the throne of God—like no one else can.

● **Embrace the opportunity you have to pray specifically for your husband.**

At this point, I'm sure you're thinking, "I do pray for my husband!" But what do those prayers amount to?

Too often our prayers are brief and ambiguous, filled with appeals for God to help or bless our husbands in their ministries. Prayers characterized by generic terms such as these could be described as anemic, trite, or even vain repetitions.

Because you know your pastor-husband best, you can pray for him like no one else can. You have the opportunity, even the responsibility, as your husband's helper, to labor in prayer for him.

How can you pray specifically for him? How can you effectively labor in prayer for your pastor-husband?

● **Let Scripture guide your prayer for your pastor-husband.**

As a young pastor's wife, I recognized my need to pray fervently for my husband. I read books that addressed how wives should pray for their husbands, and I began implementing these helpful ideas into my prayer life. I soon recognized, however, that my pastor-husband had needs specific to his life-calling that these books weren't addressing. So I began to search Scripture for how to pray specifically for my pastor-husband.

Scripture has much to say about one who is a minister of the Word. Paul's epistles include personal testimony of his view of ministry, along with instructions specific to pastors, and those instructions provide specific content for prayers for a pastor-husband. Additionally, exhortations given to all believers can be adapted to prayers that intercede for the specific needs of a pastor.

The Word of God provides the content for our prayers for our pastor-husbands. Will you join me in developing a robust pattern of prayer for that man you are called to help?

# How to Use This Resource

Pray through the various categories, personalizing the prayers based on your knowledge of your husband.

Use the blank pages to add more Scripture prayers that pertain to that topic.

Using the blank pages at the end of the book, add other categories specific to your husband's needs, along with personalized Scripture prayers that pertain to that topic.

Include the prayers of this book in your daily prayer routine, praying regularly for your pastor-husband.

Consider scheduling a block of time each week for designated prayer just for your pastor-husband. (When my husband was a pastor, I had a designated time of prayer for him on Saturdays while he was reviewing his Sunday sermon. This was, I believe, my greatest contribution to the ministry opportunities that each Sunday provided.)

# Gratitude for His Calling

- Thank You, Christ Jesus our Lord, that You have enabled my husband, because You counted him faithful, putting him into the ministry. 1 Timothy 1:12

- Thank You, Lord, that my husband became a minister according to Your stewardship which was given to him for us, to fulfill Your word. Colossians 1:25

- Thank You that You are faithful who calls him, who also will do it. 1 Thessalonians 5:24

# Faithfulness to His Calling

- I pray that he would be filled with the knowledge of Your will in all wisdom and spiritual understanding; that he might walk worthy of You, fully pleasing You, being fruitful in every good work and increasing in the knowledge of You. Colossians 1:9–10

- I pray that he would take heed to the ministry which he has received in You, that he fulfill it. Colossians 4:17

- I pray that he would compete "according to the rules," following the instructions You have given him. 2 Timothy 2:5

- I pray that as he has received the gift, he would minister it to others, as a good steward of Your manifold grace. 1 Peter 4:10

- I pray that he would be faithful until death so that You will give him the crown of life. Revelation 2:10b

# Godly Character

- I pray that my husband would be blameless, the husband of one wife, temperate, sober-minded, of good behavior, hospitable, able to teach; not given to wine, not violent, not greedy for money, but gentle, not quarrelsome, not covetous; one who rules his own house well, having his children in submission with all reverence; not a novice, lest being puffed up with pride he fall into the same condemnation as the devil. May he have a good testimony among those who are outside, lest he falls into reproach and the snare of the devil. 1 Timothy 3:2–4, 6–7

- I pray that my husband would be an example to the believers in word, in conduct, in love, in spirit, in faith, and in purity. 1 Timothy 4:12

- I pray that he would be watchful in all things, endure afflictions, do the work of an evangelist, and fulfill his ministry. 2 Timothy 4:5

# Spiritual Growth

- I pray that he would apply the truths of Your Word to his life first, before exhorting others to do so.
  2 Timothy 2:6—7

- I pray that he would give all diligence to add to his faith virtue, to virtue knowledge, to knowledge self-control, to self-control perseverance, to perseverance godliness, to godliness brotherly kindness, and to brotherly kindness love. 2 Peter 1:5—7

- I pray that he would grow in the grace and knowledge of You. To You be the glory both now and forever. Amen. 2 Peter 3:18

# Protection from Sin

---

- I pray that he would flee these things (pride and love of money) and pursue righteousness, godliness, faith, love, patience, and gentleness. That he would fight the good fight of faith, lay hold on eternal life, to which he was also called and has confessed the good confession in the presence of many witnesses. 1 Timothy 6:11—12

- I pray that he would flee youthful lusts and pursue righteousness, faith, love, and peace with those who call on You out of a pure heart. 2 Timothy 2:22

- I pray that You will establish him and guard him from the evil one. 2 Thessalonians 3:3

- I pray that my husband would be sober and vigilant, because his adversary the devil walks about like a roaring lion, seeking whom he may devour. May my husband resist him, steadfast in the faith, knowing that the same sufferings are experienced by his brotherhood in the world. 1 Peter 5:8—9

# Personal Testimony

- I pray that he would let his light so shine before men, that they may see his good works and glorify You. Matthew 5:16

- I pray that in all things he would show himself a pattern of good works; in doctrine showing integrity, reverence, incorruptibility, and sound speech that cannot be condemned; that one who is an opponent may be ashamed, having nothing evil to say of him. Titus 2:7—8

- I pray that he would shepherd Your flock which is among him, serving as an overseer, not by compulsion but willingly, not for dishonest gain but eagerly; neither as being a lord over those entrusted to him, but being an example to the flock. 1 Peter 5:2—3

# Not Distracted by the World

- I pray that he would set his mind on things above, not on things on the earth. Colossians 3:2

- I pray that he would not entangle himself with the affairs of this life, that he may please You who enlisted him as a soldier. 2 Timothy 2:4

- I pray that he would never forsake gospel ministry due to a love for this present world. 2 Timothy 4:10

- I pray that he would not love the world or the things in the world. 1 John 2:15a

# Compassion

- I pray that he would love others as You have loved him. John 15:12

- I pray that he would walk worthy of the calling with which he was called, with all lowliness and gentleness, with longsuffering, bearing with others in love, endeavoring to keep the unity of the Spirit in the bond of peace. Ephesians 4:1–3

- I pray that he, Your servant, would not quarrel but be gentle to all, able to teach, patient, in humility correcting those who are in opposition, if You perhaps will grant them repentance, so that they may know the truth. 2 Timothy 2:24–25

# Wisdom in Relationships

- I pray that he would not rebuke an older man, but exhort him as a father, younger men as brothers, older women as mothers, younger women as sisters, with all purity. I pray that he would honor widows who are really widows. 1 Timothy 5:1–3

- I pray that my husband would observe these things without prejudice, doing nothing with partiality. 1 Timothy 5:21

- I pray that my husband would not lay hands on anyone hastily, nor share in other people's sins and keep himself pure. 1 Timothy 5:22

- I pray that my husband would withdraw himself from anyone who teaches otherwise and does not consent to wholesome words, even Your words, and to the doctrine which accords with godliness. 1 Timothy 6:3, 5b

- I pray that he would avoid foolish and ignorant disputes, knowing that they generate strife. 2 Timothy 2:23

# *Sermon Preparation* part 1

- I pray that You would be with my husband's mouth and teach him what he shall say. Exodus 4:12

- I pray that You would open his eyes, that he may see wondrous things from Your law. Psalm 119:18

- I pray that You would put Your words in his mouth. Jeremiah 1:9

- I ask You to open his understanding, that he might comprehend the Scriptures. Luke 24:45

- I pray that my husband would be diligent to present himself approved to You, a worker who does not need to be ashamed, rightly dividing the word of truth. 2 Timothy 2:15

- I pray that my husband will ask You for wisdom, who gives to all liberally and without reproach. Thank You that You promise to give it to him. James 1:5

- I pray that Your good hand would be upon him and that he would prepare his heart to seek Your law, and to do it, and to teach the people Your statues and judgments. Ezra 7:9b—10

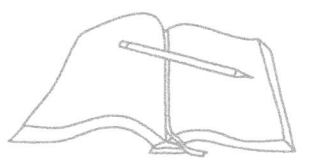

- I pray that he would take heed to himself, and to all the flock, among which the Holy Spirit has made him overseer, to shepherd Your church which You purchased with Your own blood. Acts 20:28

- I pray that he would preach You, warning every man and teaching every man in all wisdom, that he may present every man perfect in You. Colossians 1:28

- May he rebuke those who are sinning in the presence of all, that the rest also may fear. 1 Timothy 5:20

- I pray that he would command those who are rich in this present age not to be haughty, nor to trust in uncertain riches but in You, the living God, who gives us richly all things to enjoy. Let them do good, that they be rich in good works, ready to give, and willing to share. 1 Timothy 6:17—18

- O Lord, I pray that he would guard what was committed to his trust, avoiding the profane and idle babblings and contradictions of what is falsely called knowledge. 1 Timothy 6:20

- I pray that he would hold fast the pattern of sound words in faith and love which are in You. I pray that he would keep by the Holy Spirit who dwells in us that good thing which was committed to him. 2 Timothy 1:13–14

- I pray that my husband would be strong in the grace that is in You and that he will commit the things he has heard to faithful men who will be able to teach others also. 2 Timothy 2:1–2

- I pray that he would hold fast the faithful word as he has been taught, that he may be able, by sound doctrine, both to exhort and convict those who contradict. Titus 1:9

- I pray that he would speak the things which are proper for sound doctrine. Titus 2:1

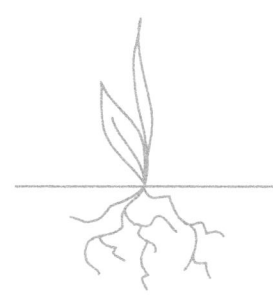

# Preaching Effectively and Boldly

- I pray that my husband would speak to people all that You command him. I pray that he would be not dismayed before their faces, lest You dismay him before them. Jeremiah 1:17

- I pray that he would stir up the gift You have given which is in him through the laying on of hands. For You have not given him the spirit of fear, but of power and of love and of a sound mind. 2 Timothy 1:6–7

- I pray that my husband would not be ashamed of Your testimony but that he would be share in the sufferings for the gospel according to Your power. 2 Timothy 1:8

- I pray that he would preach the word! May he be ready in season and out of season. May he convince, rebuke, exhort, with all longsuffering and teaching. 2 Timothy 4:2

# God's Enabling Power

- I pray that You would make all grace abound toward my husband and that he, always having all sufficiency in all things, may have an abundance for every good work. 2 Corinthians 9:8

- I pray that he would be strengthened with all might, according to Your glorious power, for all patience and longsuffering with joy. Colossians 1:11

- I pray that he would labor, striving according to Your working which works in him mightily. Colossians 1:29

- I pray that Your word may run swiftly and be glorified. 2 Thessalonians 3:1

# Handling Discouragement *part 1*

- I pray that he would be of good courage, knowing You will strengthen his heart as he hopes in You. Psalm 31:24

- I pray that he would not be cast down or disquieted, but that he would hope in You and praise You, for You are his help. Psalm 42:5

- I pray that he would set his hope in You, and not forget Your works, but would keep Your commandments. Psalm 78:7

- I pray that You would be his hiding place and his shield; I pray that he would hope in Your word. Psalm 119:114

- I pray that he would not be shaken by these afflictions. 1 Thessalonians 3:3a

- I pray that in everything he would give thanks. 1 Thessalonians 5:18a

# *Handling Discouragement* part 2

- I pray that he would remember that You who calls him are faithful, who also will do it. 1 Thessalonians 5:24

- I pray that You would comfort his heart and establish him in every good word and work.
  2 Thessalonians 2:17

- I pray that he would not grow weary in doing good.
  2 Thessalonians 3:13

- May You give him peace always in every way.
  2 Thessalonians 3:16a

# *Perseverance* part 1

---

- I pray that he would be steadfast, immovable, always abounding in Your work, knowing that his labor is not in vain in You. 1 Corinthians 15:58

- I pray that my husband would meditate on these things (reading, exhortation, and doctrine); give himself entirely to them, that his progress may be evident to all. I pray he would take heed to himself and to the doctrine and that he would continue in them, for in doing this he will save both himself and those who hear him. 1 Timothy 4:15–16

- I pray that he would endure hardship as Your good soldier. 2 Timothy 2:3

- I pray that he would endure all things for the sake of the elect, that they also may obtain the salvation which is in You with eternal glory. 2 Timothy 2:10

# *Perseverance* part 2

---

- I pray that he would continue in the things which he has learned and been assured of, knowing from whom he has learned them. 2 Timothy 3:14

- I pray that he would be watchful in all things, endure afflictions, do the work of an evangelist, and fulfill his ministry. 2 Timothy 4:5

# My Personalized Prayers

Praying for your pastor-husband is not a one-size-fits-all endeavor. You undoubtedly know of specific areas in your husband's ministry and personal life for which you are burdened to pray. Using that knowledge of his burdens and needs, add other prayer categories, along with personalized Scripture prayers that pertain to those areas.

# My Personalized Prayers

# My Personalized Prayers